CCSS **Genre** Realistic Fi

MW00682368

 Essential Questio
What do you do at your school?

Class Party

by Rachel Tandy
illustrated by Jamie Smith

Chapter 1
How Can We Celebrate? 2

Chapter 2
How Can Eve Help?. 9

Respond to Reading 12

PAIRED READ Our Classroom Rules 13

Focus On Social Studies. 16

Mrs. Lopez has a question for her class.

"What happened last week?" she asks.

"We won the spelling bee!" everyone says.

"What can we do to celebrate?"
asks Mrs. Lopez.

"We can have a party,"
Mark answers.

"That's a good idea,"
says Mrs. Lopez.

"A party at school will be fun!" says Kate.

All the children are excited. They cannot wait for the party.

Mrs. Lopez talks to the class about the party.

"We will need food and drinks for our party. How can we get those things?" asks Mrs. Lopez.

The children think about it.

"We can all bring something," says Juan.

"That's a good idea, Juan," says Mrs. Lopez.

The children take turns. Juan says he will bring drinks. Luke wants to bring apples.

"I can make popcorn,"
says Mark.

"And I can bring muffins,"
says Kate. "My mom will help
me make them."

"I can bring plates and napkins," says Max.

"I can bring the cups," Jack adds.

Chapter 2

How Can Eve Help?

Everyone is excited, but Eve does not say anything.

"What's wrong?" asks Mrs. Lopez.

"There's nothing left for me to bring!" says Eve. "I want to help, too."

Then Luke has an idea.

"We will need party hats,"
he says. "You can bring the
party hats, Eve!"

"I like party hats," says Eve. "I will make them. That's how I can help!"

"That's a good idea," says Mrs. Lopez. "If we all help out, it will be a great party!"

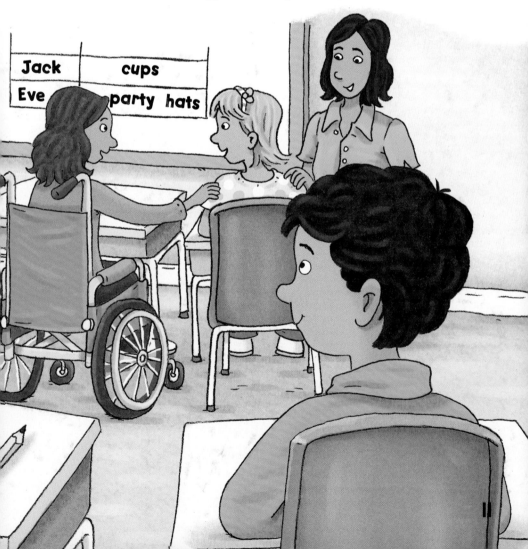

Respond to Reading

Retell

Use your own words to retell details in *Class Party.*

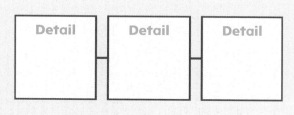

Text Evidence

1. Look at page 7. How does Mrs. Lopez keep a record of the children's ideas? Key Details

2. Look at page 9. What details tell you that Eve is sad?

   Key Details

3. How do you know that *Class Party* is realistic fiction? Genre

Our Classroom Rules

Genre Nonfiction

Compare Texts
Read about classroom rules.

We follow rules in the classroom. Rules can help us. We raise our hands to talk one at a time. Then everyone can hear what we have to say.

We share things in the classroom. We share the paper, pens, and glue. Then everyone can use them.

What rules do you have in your classroom?

Make Connections

What rules are the same in *Our Classroom Rules* and in *Class Party*?

Text to Text

Focus on
Social Studies

Purpose To learn how following the rules of a game help us have fun

What to Do

Step 1 ▶ Pick a game you like to play with your friends at school.

Step 2 ▶ Draw a chart like this one.

Rules	How they help us

Step 3 ▶ Write two rules for the game on the chart. Write how following the rules makes the game more fun.